STATUTORY MATERNITY PAY AND MATERNITY RIGHTS

Sue Morris

The Industrial Society

First published in 1995 by
The Industrial Society
Robert Hyde House
48 Bryanston Square
London W1H 7LN
Telephone: 0171–262–2401

ISBN 1 85835 229 0

British Library Cataloguing-in-Publication Data.
A catalogue record for this book is available from the British Library

Typeset by: The Midlands Book Typesetting Company, Loughborough
Printed by: Bourne Press
Cover design: Martin Bronkhorst

The Industrial Society is a Registered Charity No. 290003

Contents

1.	Introduction	1
2.	Summary of the Scheme	3
3.	Qualifying Conditions for SMP	5
4.	Scope of the Scheme	7
5.	Qualifying Service for SMP	11
6.	Working Out Average Earnings	19
7.	Stages of Pregnancy	23
8.	Maternity Pay Period	27
9.	Issues Affecting Entitlement to SMP	31
10.	What to Pay	37
11.	Manner and Time of Payments	39
12.	Notification Requirements	43
13.	Medical Evidence	47
14.	Appeals	49
15.	Records	53
16.	Mistakes, Offences & Penalties	55

17. SMP and SSP 59
18. Ante-Natal Care 63
19. Maternity Leave and the Right to Return 67
20. Maternity Leave Period 69
21. Longer Maternity Absence Period 75
22. Unfair Dismissal 85
23. Contractual Maternity Schemes and Composite Rights 87
24. Redundancy and Other Reasons 89
25. Pregnancy Discrimination and Equal Pay 95
26. Health and Safety 101
Appendices 1. Legislation Affecting SMP and Maternity Rights 107
2. Form SMP 1 109
3. State Maternity Allowance & SMP (1994/95) 111
4. Maternity Certificate 113
5. Termination Dates 115
6. Draft Example Letters 117
7. Action Checklist 121
8. Non-exhaustive List of Agents, Processes and Working Conditions 123

CHAPTER

1 Introduction

Maternity Pay and Maternity Leave were first introduced by the Employment Protection Act 1975 when employers were required to pay six weeks' maternity pay which they subsequently claimed back from the Department of Employment through the Maternity Pay Fund.

This arrangement was replaced by the Statutory Maternity Pay Scheme which was introduced on 6 April 1987 as part of the government's reforms of social security.

As a result of this maternity payments were increased to eighteen weeks, ie six weeks at a higher rate followed by twelve weeks at the standard rate, set by the State, subject to certain qualifying conditions.

Further improvements were made to the State Maternity Pay Scheme with effect from 16 October 1994 to comply with the requirements of the EC Directive on Pregnant Workers. This allows more women to be eligible for payments as a result of changes to the qualifying conditions.

The State Maternity Allowance which is paid by the Department of Social Security was largely replaced by the introduction of the

Statutory Maternity Scheme in 1987 and this too will be subject to changed qualifying conditions from the same date.

As a result of the EC Directive on Pregnant Workers, all employees will be entitled to fourteen weeks' maternity leave, regardless of their period of service or hours worked, with effect from 16 October 1994. The right to the 'longer' maternity absence period and paid time off for ante-natal care remains unchanged.

The Directive is concerned with the whole of pregnancy and maternity and the health of the child and therefore includes health and safety measures in addition to Statutory Maternity Pay and leave.

CHAPTER 2

Summary of the Scheme

SMP is operated in a similar way to Statutory Sick Pay in that it is paid by employers in the same way that wages are paid, eg weekly or monthly and is subject to deductions for national insurance and income tax under the PAYE scheme.

The amount of SMP that can be reclaimed from the State is then deducted from the National Insurance Contributions (NIC) and PAYE remittances paid to the Inland Revenue at the end of each pay period.

Up to 16 October 1994, employers were compensated for administering SMP by being able to reclaim a percentage of the SMP they paid out on top of the amount of SMP paid out. This compensation payment will not be claimable from the above date, except for small employers, who will continue to be able to claim 4%.

SMP is paid for a maximum of eighteen weeks regardless of whether the woman intends to return to work after the baby is born.

There are two rates of SMP – a higher rate and a lower rate. The higher rate is paid for six weeks and is calculated on the basis of 90% of the woman's average earnings.

The lower rate is paid for twelve weeks and is set by the State. For example, with effect from 16 October 1994 the lower rate will be £52.50.

To qualify for SMP the employee must have been continuously employed by the same employer for twenty-six weeks and her average earnings must be at or above the Lower Earnings Limit which from 6 April 1994 is set at £57.00 per week.

SMP is payable during the Maternity Pay Period (MPP) which is eighteen weeks. The earliest that SMP can be paid is eleven weeks before the Expected Week of Childbirth (EWC).

Women may choose to work past the eleven weeks before the EWC any time up to the week before the baby is due without any reduction in their entitlement to SMP. Prior to 16 October 1994, if a woman worked past the sixth week before the EWC, she lost one week of lower rate SMP for each week worked.

The woman must notify her employer, in writing if required, at least twenty-one days before she intends to stop work that she will be absent from work due to pregnancy and the expected birth of her baby. She is entitled to SMP whether or not it is her intention to return to work.

If a baby is stillborn or the woman has a miscarriage before the end of the 24th week of pregnancy then SMP is not payable.

There is a strict requirement on the woman to provide her employer with evidence of her pregnancy and her expected date of childbirth (EWC) before SMP is paid and this must be in the form of a MAT B1. See example in Appendix, Page 113.

CHAPTER 3

Qualifying Conditions for SMP

The following conditions must be met to qualify for SMP:

- she must be an 'employee';
- she must have been continuously employed for 26 weeks into the week before the 15th week prior to the expected week of confinement (QW);
- she must have average weekly earnings at or above the Lower Earnings Limit (LEL);
- she must have reached the eleventh week before the EWC or have given birth to a live child prematurely.

The above conditions will be explained more fully later in this book.

CHAPTER 4

Scope of the Scheme

Definition of Employee

Only employees are eligible for SMP.

An 'employee' is defined in Regulation 17 of the General Regulations as:

> A woman over the age of 16 whose earnings attract liability for employer's Class 1 National Insurance Contributions (NIC) or would do if her earnings were high enough, that is above the Lower Earnings Limit (LEL).

From 6 April 1994 the LEL was set at £57.00.

Definition of employer

Only 'employers' are liable to pay SMP, ie the person who is liable to pay the employer's element of the NIC.

For example, an Employment Agency will be liable to pay their temporary 'employed' staff SMP and not the organisations for whom they carry out the work, provided that they fulfil all the other qualifying conditions, eg if they have been continuously employed for twenty-six weeks at the QW. If there have been breaks between contracts then the Agency will not become liable to pay SMP but the woman may be able to claim State Maternity Allowance from the DSS.

Seasonal workers or regular casuals

An employer may well be liable to pay SMP to seasonal workers or regular casuals even if there are breaks in their service providing that they meet certain qualifying conditions.

The scope for seasonal workers or regular casuals to qualify for SMP was widened by the SMP (General) Regulations 1990 so that more people would qualify.

No written contract of employment exists

The employer will be liable for paying SMP to an employee for whom he pays NIC even where no written contract of employment has been issued to the employee.

Employee has more than one employer at the same time

A woman may have more than one employer at the same time whereby her earnings under each contract are insufficient to qualify for Class 1 National Insurance Contributions, ie they fall below the LEL. The 1979 Social Security (Contributions) Regulations allow for her earnings to be added together and treated as one single payment for NIC purposes.

Where this occurs, the employers will become liable to pay SMP. The SMP payment will be split between the employers as they agree or if they fail to agree it will be split on a pro rata basis to the amount of the woman's earnings with each employer.

Exceptions

The following categories of employee are excluded from SMP:

- women serving in Her Majesty's Forces including the Reserve Forces;
- foreign-going mariners employed by a UK employer who pays the special rate of NIC;
- mariners employed by a UK employer trading within the near continental limits are covered by the scheme except if they are outside the European Economic Areas during their MPP;
- if a woman working on the Continental Shelf is confined early or cannot be returned to the mainland when her MPP is due to start she should be treated as if she were in the UK;
- employers are only liable to pay SMP to employees for whom they are liable to pay NIC. So any employee who is not normally resident in an EC country and for whom there is no liability to pay the employer's share of the NIC will not be entitled to SMP;
- SMP is not payable for any week in which the woman goes outside the European Economic Area or is taken into legal custody or for any week afterwards.

The woman may be able to claim Maternity Allowance from the Department of Social Security so she should be given form SMP 1 and her maternity certificate MAT B1 should be returned to her. A copy of the maternity certificate should be retained by the employer.

CHAPTER 5

Qualifying Service for SMP

Whether or not the woman qualifies for SMP will depend on the period of her continuous service.

From 16 October 1994 all employees who have worked in the same job for 26 weeks, at the 15th week (QW) before the week in which the baby is due to be born (EWC), will be entitled to the higher rate of SMP for six weeks followed by the lower rate of SMP for 12 weeks.

The qualifying week

The 15th week before the expected week of childbirth (EWC) is the qualifying week. The expected date of the birth is shown on the maternity certificate (MAT B1) or some other medical document.

Example

EDC = Wednesday 17 August 1994
EWC starts on Sunday 14 August 1994
15th week before EWC starts on Sunday 1 May 1994
Her latest start date to qualify for SMP is 13 November 1993

The woman must be continuously employed into the week beginning Sunday 1 May to qualify for SMP. Even if she is employed for only one day in this week she will be deemed to have been employed into the 15th week before the EWC.

The relevant dates for the above example are marked on the calendar below:

1994 Calendar

JANUARY

M	T	W	T	F	S	S
					1	2
3	4	5	6	7	8	9
10	11	12	13	14	15	16
17	18	19	20	21	22	23
24	25	26	27	28	29	30
31						

FEBRUARY

M	T	W	T	F	S	S
	1	2	3	4	5	6
7	8	9	10	11	12	13
14	15	16	17	18	19	20
21	22	23	24	25	26	27
28						

MARCH

M	T	W	T	F	S	S
	1	2	3	4	5	6
7	8	9	10	11	12	13
14	15	16	17	18	19	20
21	22	23	24	25	26	27
28	29	30	31			

APRIL

M	T	W	T	F	S	S
				1	2	3
4	5	6	7	8	9	10
11	12	13	14	15	16	17
18	19	20	21	22	23	24
25	26	27	28	29	30	

MAY

M	T	W	T	F	S	S
						1
2	3	4	5	6	7	8
9	10	11	12	13	14	15
16	17	18	19	20	21	22
23	24	25	26	27	28	29
30	31					

JUNE

M	T	W	T	F	S	S
		1	2	3	4	5
6	7	8	9	10	11	12
13	14	15	16	17	18	19
20	21	22	23	24	25	26
27	28	29	30			

JULY

M	T	W	T	F	S	S
				1	2	3
4	5	6	7	8	9	10
11	12	13	14	15	16	17
18	19	20	21	22	23	24
25	26	27	28	29	30	31

AUGUST

M	T	W	T	F	S	S
1	2	3	4	5	6	7
8	9	10	11	12	13	14
15	16	17	18	19	20	21
22	23	24	25	26	27	28
29	30	31				

SEPTEMBER

M	T	W	T	F	S	S
			1	2	3	4
5	6	7	8	9	10	11
12	13	14	15	16	17	18
19	20	21	22	23	24	25
26	27	28	29	30		

OCTOBER

M	T	W	T	F	S	S
					1	2
3	4	5	6	7	8	9
10	11	12	13	14	15	16
17	18	19	20	21	22	23
24	25	26	27	28	29	30
31						

NOVEMBER

M	T	W	T	F	S	S
	1	2	3	4	5	6
7	8	9	10	11	12	13
14	15	16	17	18	19	20
21	22	23	24	25	26	27
28	29	30				

DECEMBER

M	T	W	T	F	S	S
			1	2	3	4
5	6	7	8	9	10	11
12	13	14	15	16	17	18
19	20	21	22	23	24	25
26	27	28	29	30	31	

The next step is to find out whether the employee has the appropriate period of continuous service.

Working out continuous service

A woman must have 26 weeks' continuous service into the qualifying week to qualify for SMP. To accumulate 26 weeks' service an employee will only have to work during any part of the first week of her employment and not a full week, ie from Sunday to Saturday in her first week.

Example

Date of starting employment: Thursday 21 July 1994;
Qualifying week (15th week before EWC): Sunday 8 January 1995.

Weeks which count

To calculate continuous service you must consider the employee's service week by week (a week ends on Saturday midnight for this purpose). The provisions of the General Regulations governing continuity of service now state that an employee must have the requisite continuous service starting from the day the employee began work and counting the weeks and calendar months.

However, as stated above, she will only have to work during any part of the first week of her employment for that week to be counted.

Working without a break

Continuous service normally means working for the same employer or an associated employer without a break but there are certain exceptions to this.

Exceptions

Regulation 11 provides that where in any week a woman is, for the whole or part of the week, absent, then those weeks will count towards her continuity of service and her service will not be broken:

- if she is incapable of work due to sickness or injury, or pregnancy, provided that it does not last longer than 26 consecutive weeks;
- statutory maternity leave;

- if there is a temporary cessation of work (not subject to any specific time limit);
- if there is a custom or arrangement that she may be absent from work whilst being regarded as continuing in employment.

Seasonal or regular casuals

Many employers employ seasonal staff during the year who may return in the following year. Other employers employ 'regular casuals' working, for example, in hotels or theatres, who work on a casual basis, often with short gaps between each period of service. These workers may not break their continuity of service if they can show that there has only been a temporary cessation of work.

Also, following the Statutory Maternity Pay (General) Amendment Regulations 1990, provided that certain requirements are met, continuity of employment will be maintained for SMP purposes even if the pregnant woman does not return to the original employer before going on maternity leave.

These qualifying conditions are:

- the pregnant woman's employer customarily offers her work for a fixed period of not more than 26 consecutive weeks;
- the employer offers work for a similar spell on two or more occasions in a year for periods which do not overlap;
- the employer offers work to those individuals who had worked for him during the last or a recent period of this type of employment but the pregnant woman concerned is absent during the qualifying week, wholly or partly because of pregnancy, childbirth disease, or bodily or mental disablement.

To retain her rights to SMP in the above circumstances, the employee will still have to satisfy the earnings rule and notification requirements.

Although a woman must show that she has 26 weeks' continuous service working back from the 15th week before her EWC, the Tribunals will take note of the whole of her employment history, not just the most recent 26 weeks, to determine whether any break in service was of a temporary nature (*Flack v. Kodak Limited 1985 IRLR 443*).

Working alternate weeks, ie one week on and one week off, during a year does not break continuity since that has been seen as the employee being absent on the alternate weeks by reason of a 'custom or arrangement' and therefore her contract of employment is regarded as continuing during her 'off' weeks for the purposes of continuity of employment. (*Lloyds Bank Limited v. Secretary of State for Employment 1979 IRLR 41.*) This case is open to criticism.

Agency workers

If an employee has done some work for the same agency in each of the 26 weeks into the QW then she will satisfy the continuous service requirement.

Even if she has not worked for complete weeks for the agency, continuity will not necessarily be broken. For example, if work was offered but the woman was unavailable due to sickness, injury or pregnancy then continuity will not be broken.

If the agency has no work for the woman during the QW but she is available for work and in fact works for the agency following the QW but before maternity absence starts then she will satisfy the qualifying conditions.

If the employee had intended to go on working during the QW but was prevented from doing so through sickness, then providing she returns to work for that agency within 26 weeks of stopping, she will be regarded as having worked into the QW and will therefore qualify for SMP.

Spasmodic employment

Some employees, such as supply teachers, work only as and when required and their breaks between employment will not necessarily break continuity of employment.

The same rules as for agency workers apply except that if the employee is sick through the qualifying week, the employee can be regarded as having worked in the QW even if she does not return to work because of sickness before the start of her maternity absence.

Trade disputes

If a woman goes on strike for any week or part week then the period during which she does not work will not break continuity but those weeks in which the stoppage occurred will not count towards the computation of her length of service. This does not apply if the employee can show that she was 'locked out' or she had no direct interest in the strike.

Hours of work

There are no hours requirements to qualify for SMP although conditions such as earnings level, length of continuous service and confirmation of the state of pregnancy must be satisfied.

Continuous service with the same employer

The continuity rules provide that a woman must have continuous service with the same employer; however there are certain exceptions:

Exceptions

- where there is a transfer of a business or undertaking to another employer (see Transfer of Undertakings (Protection of Employment) Regulations 1981);
- where by Statute or local by-laws, one corporate body takes over from another as employer;
- where the employer dies and personal representatives or trustees continue to employ the woman;
- where there is a change in the partners, personal representatives or trustees who employ the woman;
- where the woman changes employment to an 'associated employer', ie if one is a company of which the other directly or indirectly has control;
- if the woman is a teacher and leaves her employment in one school and moves to another school maintained by the same local authority (this equally applies where the Governors of that school are the teacher's employers rather than the local education authority).

CHAPTER 6

Working Out Average Earnings

To be entitled to SMP an woman's average weekly earnings for the period of eight weeks ending with the last pay day immediately before the end of the QW must be at or above the LEL (Lower Earnings Limit) (from 6 April 1994 this figure was set at £57.00) – Section 50(3) of the Act. See Appendix 3 Page 111.

Earnings which count towards SMP

Regulation 20 defines what earnings count in this calculation. They include all gross earnings which attract liability for National Insurance Contributions (NIC) including:

- bonuses;
- overtime payments;
- back payments of wages;
- SSP paid in that period;
- any arrears of pay paid under an Order for Re-instatement or Re-engagement after a finding of Unfair Dismissal;
- any sum paid under a protective award.

The following are examples of those payments that are excluded:

- redundancy payments;
- re-imbursement of business expenses;

- payments in kind for provision of board and lodging;
- pension payments.

Calculating average weekly earnings

All earnings should be added together over the eight weeks up to and including the last pay day before the end of the QW. The gross figure should be used before any deductions have been made, eg for Income Tax and National Insurance Contributions.

If a woman is unfairly dismissed before the QW and the Industrial Tribunal orders re-instatement or re-engagement then you may be liable to pay SMP. Contact your local DSS office for advice.

If the woman has her baby before the end of the QW and this results in a live birth (as opposed to a stillbirth or a miscarriage) use her average weekly earnings over the last eight weeks ending with the last complete week before the week in which the baby was born.

For weekly paid employees

If the woman is normally paid weekly on the same day each week, for example Friday, take her earnings on the eight pay days ending with the last pay day before the end of the QW and divide the result by eight to produce a weekly average.

Example

Pay week	1	2	3	4	5	6	7	8	End of QW
Earnings	£90	£95	£105	£90	£95	£90	£110	£115	19 November 94

Average weekly earnings = £790 ÷ 8 = £98.75.

For calendar monthly paid employees

If the woman is paid calendar monthly and the normal pay day is the last day of each month, add together the payments made on the last normal pay day before the end of the QW and any other payments made since, but not including, the last pay day to fall at least eight weeks earlier than that one. Multiply the total by six and divide by fifty-two.

Example

Employee paid on the last day of the month.
The end of the QW is Saturday 19 November 1994.

Add together the earnings from 1 September 1994 to 31 October 1994, ie the last pay day before the end of the QW.

See diagram below:

August	September	October	November
Pay day 31 Aug	Pay day 30 Sep	Pay day 31 Oct	End of QW 19 Nov

In this example payments made on 30 September and 31 October should be included.

Payments made at other intervals

Where an employee is paid at other intervals, add together the payments made on the last pay day before the end of the QW and any other payments made since, but not including, the last pay day to fall at least eight weeks earlier than that one.

The period over which the earnings are averaged begins on the day after the pay day stated above and ends with the last pay day before the end of the QW. If this period includes odd days then they should be counted as one seventh of a week each.

Example

The QW weeks ends on Saturday 19 November 1994.
The woman was paid on 19 October, 31 August and 27 July 1994.

Add together the payments made on 19 October and 31 August 1994. The period over which these earnings should be averaged is 28 July to 19 October inclusive which is twelve weeks.

Employment with associated employers

If two or more employments are treated as continuous and the eight week averaging period falls in more than one employment then you should treat the earnings from each employment as if they had all been paid by the last employer in the period.

Rounding of payment

The calculation of the higher rate of SMP may produce an odd fraction of a penny. If this occurs you should round up to the next whole penny. Rounding should only be done after the total weekly payment at the higher rate has been worked out.

CHAPTER

7 Stages of Pregnancy

The Act in section 46(2)(c) makes it clear that a woman must actually still be pregnant at the eleventh week before the EWC or have given birth to a live baby before that date.

Baby born before the EWC

If the baby is born earlier than the EWC but after the eleventh week before the EWC then payment of SMP will not be affected.

It should continue to be paid in the normal way as if the baby had been born on the due date and should continue to be paid until the entitlement ceases.

Baby born before the QW

If the baby is born before the fifteenth week before the EWC then the woman will be due her SMP.

The conditions for SMP are modified and these are set out in Regulation 4(2)(a) and (b):

- she must, if reasonably practicable, give notice of the date when the baby was born within twenty-one days of the birth;

- the twenty-six weeks' continuous service rule will be regarded as satisfied if she would have been continuously employed for at least twenty-six weeks at the QW but for the early birth;
- the period over which the earnings rule is applied and the average weekly earnings are calculated by reference to the eight weeks ending with the week before the week in which the baby was born.

Example

Date of starting employment is 4 June 1994.
EWC is 27 November 1994.
QW is 14 August 1994.
Intended date of stopping work is 23 September 1994.
Baby is born on 11 August 1994.

At QW, 14 August 1994, the woman would have had twenty-six weeks' continuous service.

See diagram:

Jan.	Feb.	Mar.	Apr.	May	June	July	Aug.	Sept.	Oct.	Nov.	Dec.
					4 June started work		11 Aug baby born	23 Sept intended to stop work		27 Nov EWC	

14 Aug
QW

Baby born after the QW but before 11th week before EWC

If the woman has the baby before the eleventh week but after the QW then she remains entitled to SMP in the same way as normal except that she must comply with the notice rules stated above. Her MPP will then be the period of eighteen weeks beginning with the week after the week in which she had her baby.

Twins or multiple births

A woman is only entitled to one payment of SMP regardless of the number of babies which are born. She will however be entitled to Child Allowance for each baby.

More than one contract with the same employer or a different employer

If the woman has more than one contract which attracts liability for Class 1 NIC and she satisfies all the other conditions she will be entitled to SMP under each separate contract whether from the same employer or from different employers for the birth of that child.

Miscarriage or stillbirth before the 11th week before her EWC

If a baby is stillborn or the woman has a miscarriage before the end of the twenty-fourth week of pregnancy SMP is not payable although she may be entitled to Statutory Sick Pay (SSP).

CHAPTER

8 Maternity Pay Period

Definition of Employee

- SMP cannot be paid earlier than the start of the Maternity Pay Period (MPP);
- this cannot be earlier than the eleventh week before the EWC if the woman has stopped work by that date;
  she can stop work at the start of the fourteenth week before the EWC but cannot be paid her SMP any earlier than the eleventh week before her EWC – Section 47 of the Act and Regulation 2;
- the woman has the choice of continuing to work up to the week before the week in which the baby is due to be born and she will still be entitled to the maximum eighteen weeks' SMP.

Sickness absence prior to maternity leave

If the woman works past the sixth week before the EWC and she falls sick, then she will be entitled to return to work provided that the sickness absence is not related to her pregnancy. If the sickness absence is related to her pregnancy, then she will automatically start her maternity leave.

Working for another employer during the MPP

If a woman works for another employer before the baby is born, the employer who employed her at the QW will still be liable to pay SMP.

If she works for another employer after she has had the baby and while SMP is still due then liability to pay SMP will cease on the Saturday of the week in which she starts work for any other employer.

It is the employee's responsibility to tell her former employer that she is working for someone else.

MPP starts and then she returns to work for her employer

Once the woman's MPP starts and she receives SMP her eighteen weeks will run.

If for some reason she comes back to work for her employer during her MPP then no SMP will be payable during any week in which that work is done. Her eighteen week period will continue to run and she will lose a week's SMP for each week in which some work was done.

Example

MPP starts at the eleventh week before the EWC.

The woman receives two weeks' SMP then returns to work for two days in week three but thereafter does no more work. She will receive no SMP in week three and SMP should be paid again in week four, which will be the third week in which the higher rate is paid. She will only be entitled to receive eleven weeks SMP at the lower rate which means that her overall entitlement to SMP will be seventeen weeks.

MPP Broken

11	10	9	8	7	6	5	4	3	2	1	EWC
H/R SMP 1	H/R SMP 2	Works for 2 days	H/R SMP 3	H/R SMP 4	H/R SMP 5	H/R SMP 6	L/R SMP 7	L/R SMP 8	L/R SMP 9	L/R SMP 10	L/R SMP 11

Nightshift workers

Any work done on a nightshift which extends over midnight is treated as having been done entirely on the first of the two days.

CHAPTER 9

Issues Affecting Entitlement to SMP

There are a number of issues which affect entitlement, some of which have already been mentioned.

No liability to pay SMP

A woman will not be entitled to SMP under the following conditions:

Not employed at the QW

A woman who is not employed by you at any time during the QW is not entitled to SMP. She will be entitled to SMP if she ceases employment with you after the QW.

Twenty-six weeks' continuous employment rule not satisfied

Any woman who has not been or cannot be treated as having been continuously employed by you for at least twenty-six weeks into the QW is not entitled to SMP.

Earnings rule not satisfied

A woman whose average weekly earnings are below the LEL is not entitled to SMP.

Late notification

An employee who does not give you notice at an acceptable time of the date when she will stop work will not be entitled to SMP. See Chapter 12 on Notification Requirements.

No medical evidence

If a woman fails to provide medical evidence of her EWC within an acceptable period she is not entitled to SMP. See Chapter 13 on Medical Evidence.

Abroad outside the European Economic Area

If a woman is abroad outside the European Economic Area at any time in the first week of her MPP she will not be entitled to SMP at any time even when she returns to the UK.

Legal custody

If a woman is in legal custody at any time during the first week of her MPP she will not be entitled to SMP for any time during her MPP even if she is released later unless the sentence is suspended.

Legal custody means that a person is detained, usually arrested or in prison. Voluntarily helping police with their enquiries does not constitute being in legal custody and a woman in these circumstances would be entitled to SMP.

What to do if an employee is not entitled to SMP

If a woman is not entitled to SMP then she should be provided with a completed SMP 1 form, see Appendix 2 Page 109.

This should be done within seven days of your decision not to pay SMP as these forms are needed to claim State Maternity Allowance (SMA) from the DSS.

Form SMP 1 provides an explanation to the woman and the DSS as to why she is not receiving SMP from her employer and tells her how to claim SMA.

If an employer decides that no SMP or no further SMP is payable then he has a duty to inform the employee of this decision and the reasons why, in writing, to help her when submitting a claim to the DSS for state benefit such as Maternity Allowance or sickness/invalidity benefit.

This information is already included in form SMP 1 and the simplest way for the employer to comply is to give a copy of this form to the employee. The information that must be provided is:

- the employee goes into legal custody or prison;
- the employee goes outside the European Economic Area;
- date of the last week SMP was paid;
- total number of weeks in the MPP for which SMP would have been paid.

Any maternity certificates held should also be returned to the woman and a copy kept by the employer.

Liability to pay SMP ceases

An employer's liability to pay SMP ceases when:

Maximum entitlement paid

When the woman has received a maximum entitlement of eighteen weeks' SMP her entitlement will cease. Remember that if her MPP starts and then she comes back to work for any week or part week, that week's SMP is lost. Her MPP cannot be extended once it has started.

Employee goes outside the European Economic Area

Liability to pay SMP ends with the last complete week within the MPP before the woman goes outside the European Economic Area. SMP is not payable for any week in which the woman is outside the EC or for any week thereafter.

Employee is taken into legal custody

Liability to pay SMP ends with the last complete week within the MPP before the woman gets taken into legal custody. SMP is not payable for any week in which the woman is in legal custody or for any week thereafter.

Employee dies

Liability to pay SMP ends on the Saturday of the week in which the employee dies.

Other matters affecting entitlement

The contract ends

As long as the woman satisfies all the qualifying conditions then SMP is payable even if her contract of employment terminates at the start of her maternity absence. This is in contrast with SSP where liability to pay SSP ceases when the contract ends.

Contract ended to avoid liability for SMP

Where an employer deliberately terminates a woman's contract of employment before the QW to avoid liability for paying SMP, Regulation 3 provides that the employer shall become liable to pay for SMP. The woman must have a minimum of eight weeks' continuous service at the date of her dismissal.

In such circumstances she will be deemed to have been employed up to the QW and her average earnings will be calculated by reference to her normal weekly earnings for the period of eight weeks ending with her last pay day before she was dismissed.

CHAPTER 10

What to Pay

Rates of SMP

There are two rates of SMP – higher rate and a lower rate – set out in section 48 of the Act:

Higher Rate

This is paid at 90% of the woman's average weekly earnings for the first six weeks of the MPP.

Average weekly earnings are calculated in exactly the same way as described on page 20.

Lower rate

The amount of the lower rate is set by the State by Regulation and is reviewed in April each year. The rate is £52.50 for those women who were expecting a baby on or after 16 October 1994.

Change of lower rate SMP

If SMP is being paid when a new lower rate becomes operative then the new rate should be paid from the start of the week in which the change occurs.

Deductions from SMP

SMP is subject to PAYE income tax and NIC. Any other lawful deductions can also be made, eg pension contributions, trade union subscriptions, deductions under Attachment of Earnings Orders – Schedule 4 Paragraph 10 of the Act. No deduction for SMA should be made from SMP.

Offsetting SMP against other contractual payments

Any contractual payments, ie wages, maternity pay or sick pay paid to a woman on a day when SMP is due will offset any SMP and vice versa.

For example, if a woman receives any contractual remuneration for a week in which SMP is due, even though she did not work for you, then this will discharge any liability to pay SMP. The same rule will apply if you make payments under an Occupational Maternity Scheme or Sick Pay Scheme.

Note that holiday pay which has accrued to the woman and which is paid to her at the start of her maternity absence will not offset SMP.

CHAPTER 11

Manner and Time of Payments

Manner of payments

SMP should be paid in exactly the same way as the woman's wages were normally paid, eg by credit transfer, cheque or cash. It cannot be paid in kind or as board and lodging, or by way of service.

Lump sum payments

The DSS does not intend SMP to be paid in one lump sum and the Act and the Regulations define SMP in terms of a weekly rate. The present SMA is paid on a weekly basis.

There is, however, nothing in law to prevent an employer from choosing to pay SMP in a lump sum but there may be problems. For example:

- NIC – National Insurance Contributions will be due at the time of payment on the whole amount and must not be spread over the MPP;
- Overpayments – if the employer has already paid SMP and the woman returns to work in the MPP or goes to work for another employer after the baby is born during the MPP she will have been overpaid and the employer will have to repay the deductions which have been made from the NICs.

Time of payments

Normal pay day

SMP should be paid at the time when wages would have been paid.

This will normally be set down in the Principal Statement of Main Terms and Conditions of Employment or agreed informally or that which is normal practice. In other words, normal payroll practice should be followed.

No normal pay/no agreement

Where there is no agreement as to when wages are paid or no normal practice Regulation 29 (1) provides that SMP should be paid on the last day of the calendar month.

Paid through an agent

SMP can be paid through an insurance company, friendly society or payroll service to any third party.

The employer is legally responsible for ensuring that the payment is made according to the Rules including those about deductions of PAYE and NIC.

Woman unable to act for herself

If medical evidence is received that the woman cannot act for herself then arrangements should be made to pay the SMP to her husband, next of kin etc.

If there is no obvious person to whom to make the payment, then contact the local DSS and they will appoint someone to handle her SMP.

Payment after a formal decision

If the employer had originally refused to pay SMP and either the Adjudicating Officer (AO), Social Security Appeal Tribunal or Social Security Commissioner has given a formal decision that the woman is entitled to SMP then time limits are laid down in Regulation 29:

- once notified of the decision and there is no appeal or right of appeal SMP must be paid no later than the first normal pay day after the time allowed for an appeal to expire (this will be given in the written decision); or
- if the application is made for leave to appeal and this is refused SMP becomes payable no later than the first normal pay day after notice of refusal is received. If the payroll procedures make it impossible to pay on that date the woman must be paid on the next pay day.

Issuing the P45

If the woman is not returning to work after she has had her baby then her employer should issue the P45 with the last payment of SMP. Issuing a P45 normally indicates termination of employment but may not always do so.

Please note that any agreement which purports to modify, limit or exclude any employment protection rights will be void under section 140 EPCA. Such an arrangement will not stop a woman who has the right of return from exercising her statutory rights.

It may be wise to write a letter to the woman obtaining her agreement that her contract will terminate by mutual consent on that date. If the employee agrees to this arrangement her contract will be deemed to have terminated by mutual agreement on that date.

Recoupment

As from 4 September 1994 employers may recoup 92% of the amount of SMP paid by deducting that amount from the total NIC due to the Collector of Taxes for all employees.

If SMP has been paid in one tax year and has not been recovered by the end of that tax year the employer should contact the DSS before any action is taken.

Small employers' dispensation

For the tax year 1994/1995 employers who pay £20,000 or less each year in gross National Insurance Contributions will be able to claim back 100% of SMP.

There is also the right to recoup a percentage of the total of SMP paid to all employees. This percentage is set each year by Regulation and for the year 1994/1995 'small employers' are entitled to recover 4%. This amount may be deducted in the tax month in which SMP is paid or later.

CHAPTER

12 Notification Requirements

Proper notice of maternity absence

The Act, section 46(4), lays down the rules that an employee must follow in notifying her employer of her pregnancy to become entitled to SMP.

The employer may require the employee to provide notification in writing – see section 46(5). This is advisable and should be set down in the employer's Maternity Policy as one of the requirements for SMP.

The Act states that the woman:

- must give her employer notice that she is going to be absent from work because she is pregnant at least twenty-one days before her absence from work is due to begin or as soon as is reasonably practicable; and
- will normally give this notice in person but she may get someone else to give it.

Less than 21 days' notice given

It is for the employer to decide whether to accept that it was not reasonably practicable for an employee to give twenty-one days' notice of the date she intends to stop work.

If her reason is not acceptable she can be refused payment.

Advice to all pregnant employees

It would be advisable to inform all pregnant employees of the twenty-one days' notice requirement and check with them the date when notice should be given to you.

Employers may wish to give them a pro-forma letter with the date already written in and get them to fill in their details.

If a woman queries a refusal to give her SMP she may ask for a written statement and she can appeal to the Adjudication Officer (AO) – see Chapter on Appeals on page 49.

Notifying change of circumstances in the MPP

It is the woman's responsibility to inform her employers of the following if they occur during her MPP and she is being paid SMP:

- that she has started work for another employer after her baby is born if it is one who did not employ her during the QW;
- that she is going abroad outside the European Economic Area;
- that she has been taken into legal custody.

Draft letter to give to a woman at the start of her maternity leave

Name and address of employer

Date

Dear

As at   1994 you will be starting your maternity leave and we will be paying you Statutory Maternity Pay for the next 14/18 weeks.

Will you please let us know if:

1 you go to work for another employer after your SMP payments begin and while you are still receiving SMP from us;
2 you go abroad outside the European Economic Area either at the start of your maternity leave or at any time before or after the baby is born while you are receiving SMP;
3 if you are taken into legal custody at any time.

It may affect your entitlement to SMP if any of the above situations occur and we will therefore need to know.

Yours sincerely

CHAPTER 13

Medical Evidence

The employer will need evidence of the date the baby is due to work out whether SMP is payable. (Regulation 22.)

This must be in the form of a Maternity Certificate (MAT B1) as set out in the Medical Evidence Regulations (see Appendix 4 on Page 113).

Employees will need to know exactly what evidence will be required and when they will need to produce it.

The Maternity Certificate (MAT B1) cannot be issued any earlier than the fourteenth week before the EWC unless it shows that the baby was born earlier.

It must be given to the employer no later than the end of the third week of the MPP but this can be extended to a maximum of thirteen weeks from the start of the MPP as long as the employer accepts the woman's reason for not producing it earlier.

Until the woman gives her employer this medical evidence, SMP cannot be paid. It cannot be paid under any circumstances if medical evidence is not provided by the end of the thirteenth week into the MPP.

CHAPTER

14 Appeals

Written statement

If it is decided not to pay SMP for any reason then the reason should be explained to the woman. If she does not agree she has the right to ask her employer for a written statement regarding:

- the weeks in the maternity leave that the employer regards himself as liable for SMP, if any;
- how much SMP the woman is entitled to for each of these weeks;
- why the employer does not regard himself liable to pay SMP for the other weeks.

She can ask for this written statement at any time and if the request is reasonable it must be given to her within a reasonable time (Schedule 4 Paragraph 7 of the Act).

Formal decision of the AO

If the woman does not agree with her employer's decision not to pay she can ask the Adjudication Officer (AO) for a formal decision. She will be expected to have asked for a written statement from her employer first.

DSS officers may also ask AO's for formal decisions.

The employer has no right to ask the AO for a decision. He must decide whether or not to pay SMP. Only the employee or DSS officer has the right to apply to the AO.

Neither party will appear in person before the AO but both will be able to submit written representations and any other supporting evidence, copies of which will be sent to both parties.

A formal decision will be sent by the AO to both parties and if the decision is that SMP is payable it must be paid by the fixed tim unless the employer appeals.

Decision by Social Security Appeals Tribunal

Either the employer or the employee has the right to appeal to the Social Security Appeals Tribunal. Both parties have the right to appear before this body and to be represented.

There is a right of appeal from this Tribunal only on a point of law to the Social Security Commissioners. These create precedents and the reported decisions are held at local DSS offices.

Review by AO

If new facts come to light which affect a decision the AO can review it. He will then issue a formal decision and this too can be appealed against.

Enforcement

Failure to comply in time with the decision of the AO, Tribunals or Commissioner can result in prosecution by the DSS.

Decisions of the Secretary of State

There are some decisions which only the Secretary of State for Soci Services is empowered to make. In practice these are made by senic officials of the DSS and there is a right to appeal to the High Court on a point of law.

These decisions are binding on AO's, Tribunals and Commissioners.

They concern the following issues:

- whether employment is to be treated as continuous;
- whether separate contracts are to be treated as one;
- whether an employer can receive NIC compensation on SMP;
- whether a person is, or was, an employee and the period of that employment;
- whether the employer is entitled to recover any SMP payments and if so, what;
- whether two employers are to be treated as one for SMP purposes.

CHAPTER 15

Records

Employers are required to keep the following records for at least three years after the tax year to which the records relate and they must be kept in such a way as to be accessible to DSS Inspectors:

- records of dates of maternity leave notified by employees;
- records of any weeks within the MPP for which SMP was not paid, with reasons;
- any maternity certificate (MAT B1) given by the employee to whom SMP has been paid;
- copies of any MAT B1 forms where the originals have been returned, for example, where liability has ended.

The DSS has produced an SMP record sheet, SMP 2, which may be used. Commercial SMP record keeping systems may also be used.

Other records useful to keep are:

- details of notification rules and dates on which employees notified their employer – useful if the employee disagrees with the decision not to pay because of late notification;
- copies of any current applications for decisions from or appeals to the AO, Tribunal or Commissioner and a copy of each decision with a note of the date it was received;
- a record of the calculation of the eight weeks' average earnings and calculations for higher rate SMP.

CHAPTER 16

Mistakes, Offences and Penalties

General

If a mistake is made it should be corrected by correcting the records, payments and deductions from NICs, unless it is in an earlier tax year, and the local DSS office should be informed. It is important to tell the DSS office because they may have under- or over-paid a State benefit.

If SMP has been paid in a lump sum the employer may be required to re-pay any overpaid amount.

SMP 1 issued by mistake

If a SMP 1 form has been issued and it is realised that it is incorrect and SMP should have been paid, the employer should immediately tell the woman and her DSS office so that State benefit is not paid in error. If the employer does not know her local office then he should tell his own DSS office and they will pass the information on.

Mistakes in records

Current tax year

If the correct amount of SMP has been paid but a mistake has been made in the records, a line should be drawn through the original figure, so that it can still be read, and the correct figure inserted.

Previous tax years

If mistakes are spotted in the records once the end-of-year returns have been sent to the Inspector of Taxes, the employer may still adjust returns as long as they are still held locally. Once the returns have been sent to Newcastle, the employer should contact the local DSS office for advice.

Mistakes in recovery

Current tax year

If the employer has recovered too much or too little from the NIC payments this should be corrected by decreasing or increasing the next payment to the Collector of Taxes or the payment of any end-of-year balance due.

Previous tax years

The error should not be corrected by decreasing or increasing the next monthly payment. The same applies when contributions for a year are incorrect for any other reason.

Instead the mistake should be reported to your local DSS office fo advice.

SMP wrongly paid

Tell the local DSS office if SMP has been paid when it should not have been.

The DSS will need the relevant details of the employee and the period concerned and the employee will have to complete a form which will enable her to claim State benefit.

If SMP was due but was paid at too high a rate the DSS do not need to be told. The mistake should be corrected in the maternity and wages records and any money that has been wrongly deducted or otherwise recovered must be paid back to the Inland Revenue Accounts Office.

Not enough SMP paid

If too little SMP has been paid and form SMP 1 has been issued, the employer must contact the DSS office because they may have been paying State benefit when in fact it was not due.

If SMP 1 has not been issued there is no need to tell the DSS.

Arrears of SMP must be paid to the woman and recorded in the normal way on her current P11 and wage records like any other SMP payments. You should correct the woman's personal maternity record as well.

DSS Inspector finds a mistake

If the employer agrees with the DSS Inspector that a mistake has been made then it must be corrected.

If the employer disagrees the Inspector may ask the AO for a formal decision and the employer need do no more until that decision has been received. You may appeal against this decision as previousl described.

Offences and penalties

There are a number of criminal offences laid down in the Regulation for which the following penalties are prescribed:

- failure to pay SMP within the time allowed when an AO, Tribuna or Commissioner has given a formal decision – for any one offence, a fine not exceeding £400;
- failure to provide information when requested in writing to do so to AO, Tribunal, Commissioner – for any one offence, a fine not exceeding £400 and for continued failure a fine of up to £40 for each day of failure;
- failure to keep the required records in connection with SMP – for any one offence a fine not exceeding £400 and for continued failure to keep such records a further fine of up to £40 for each day of failure;
- producing false documentation in connection with recovery of SMP payments or NIC – fine not exceeding £2000 or term of imprisonment not exceeding three months or both.

CHAPTER 17

SMP and SSP

The disqualifying period for SSP

The disqualifying period for Statutory Sick Pay (SSP) will mirror the woman's MPP which can start at any time from the eleventh week before the EWC to the week before the EWC.

No link between SMP and SSP

There is no linking period between SSP and SMP unlike the rule relating to State Maternity Allowance where there is a fifty-seven-day linking period and if during the fifty-seven days after a woman has claimed SMA she falls sick she is not entitled to SSP but must claim State Sickness Benefit.

This means that once SMP payments cease if the woman falls sick and is still under a contract of employment with the employer she may be entitled to SSP in the ordinary way.

Woman falls sick before or at the start of the MPP

If the woman gives proper notice and complies with the medical evidence requirements and falls sick before or at the start of her MPP then she will be entitled to SMP and her SSP will cease, if she is in receipt of SSP.

No notice of MPP

If a woman falls sick before the sixth week before the EWC but has given no notice of the start of her maternity leave, or gives notice that she intends to stop work past the sixth week before the EWC, then provided the sickness is not pregnancy related she may continue to claim SSP, if appropriate, and return to work following the period of sickness.

If the sickness absence is pregnancy related then her entitlement to SSP will cease and she should be transferred to SMP.

Employee returns during the MPP and falls sick within the MPP

If a woman returns to work for the employer who is paying her SMP after her baby is born but still within the MPP, then she will not be entitled to SMP for those weeks. However, if she falls sick within the MPP then the employer cannot pay SSP because she is still within the disqualifying period.

The employer should pay her SMP for the remainder of her sickness within the MPP. Once the MPP has finished, and if the woman is still sick, then she may be able to claim SSP.

Action required

Your SMP Scheme

You should tell all your female employees about the SMP Scheme and in particular:

- the rules about notifying you about their maternity absence;
- when they can choose to start their maternity leave and get SMP;
- what medical evidence you need;
- what they must notify you about during their maternity leave, for example if they go abroad outside the European Economic Area.

SMP 1 and SMP 2 record sheets

You will need to get forms SMP 1 and SMP 2 record sheets from your local DSS.

Tables to help you work out the QW will have been included with other information that has been sent to you in booklet CA36 (SMP 55).

CHAPTER 18

Ante-natal Care

The right to time off for ante-natal care

The right to time off for ante-natal care was first introduced in the Employment Act 1980 section 13 by incorporating a new section (31A) of the Employment Protection (Consolidation) Act 1978.

Section 31 A(1) states 'An employee who is pregnant and who has on the advice of a registered medical practitioner, registered midwife or registered health visitor, made an appointment to attend at any place for the purpose of receiving ante-natal care . . . has the right not to be unreasonably refused time off during her working hours to enable her to keep the appointment.'

No service qualification needed

There is no service qualification or minimum working hours requirement for this right.

There are two distinct rights

- the right not to be unreasonably refused time off for ante-natal care during working hours;
- the right to be paid for that period of absence.

Conditions for entitlement to these rights

To qualify for paid time off for the first appointment:

- the woman must be pregnant; and
- must have made an appointment to receive ante-natal care on the advice of a doctor, midwife or health visitor.

To qualify for paid time off for the second and subsequent appointments:

- she must produce for her employer, if requested, a certificate from her doctor, midwife or health visitor stating that she is pregnant and an appointment card or other document showing that an appointment has been made.

What ante-natal care actually means

Ante-natal care is not defined in the Act and it may vary with the medical condition of the woman.

Norman Tebbitt, when he was Secretary of State for Employment, stated in the House of Commons debates on this section that it was intended to cover care administered by non-medical people such as relaxation classes run by the National Childbirth Trust.

He expected that the woman would be absent on about four or five occasions.

In the case of *Gregory v. Tudsbury Ltd. (1982) IRLR 267* the Tribunal held that the term 'ante-natal care' was wide enough to cover relaxation classes.

When is it reasonable to refuse time off?

The Act envisages that there will be occasions when it will be reasonable for the employer to refuse time off because the right is 'not to be unreasonably refused' time off.

In *Gregory v. Tudsbury Limited*, the Tribunal thought that it might be reasonable to refuse time off if the employee could make an appointment outside working hours, if, for example, a woman works only in the mornings and could attend ante-natal clinics/relaxation classes in the afternoons.

Apart from situations such as this it is difficult to see how a refusal could be reasonable since the appointment will have been made on the advice of the doctor, midwife or health visitor as per the Act.

Re-arrangement of working hours

A woman does not have to re-arrange her working hours so that she can attend the clinic outside these hours nor is she obliged to make up her lost time.

In the case of *Edgar v. Giorgione Inns Limited COIT 1803/13* it was held that the employer was liable for twenty-two hours' pay for five visits to an ante-natal clinic.

Entitlement to pay for the time off

Once an employer has allowed time off the woman is automatically entitled to be paid during her absence unless she fails to comply with her employer's request for a medical certificate or the appointment card or other medical documentation.

This means that the employer is obliged to pay her for the 'time needed to keep her appointment' which could be considerably longer than the appointment itself.

In *Dhamrait v. United Biscuits Limited (Unreported)* the Industrial Tribunal held that Mrs Dhamrait was entitled to be paid for the whole of her shift even though she had only expected to miss the first hour. The appointment actually lasted longer than she had expected which together with the unavailability of transport meant that she was actually absent for the whole of her shift.

An appointment actually has to have been made

The way the Statute is phrased leaves it open to the Industrial Tribunal to interpret this provision literally and hold that where a woman has not actually made an appointment she is not entitled to time off.

Infertility treatment

The right in law to time off for ante-natal care does not extend to employees, whether male or female, seeking time off to attend an appointment for treatment of infertility. However, it should be borne in mind that refusal of reasonable time off for such treatment may lead to an employee resigning her employment and claiming constructive dismissal or sex discrimination.

CHAPTER 19

Maternity Leave and the Right to Return

To comply with the requirements of the EC Directive on Pregnant Workers, Part III of the Employment Protection (Consolidation) Act 1978 has been amended by the Trade Union Reform and Employment Rights Act 1993, Section 23, to give the right to all women to have fourteen weeks' maternity leave and to return to work regardless of their hours of work or their length of continuous service.

The right to the new maternity leave period takes effect from 16 October 1994 and will co-exist with the existing right of women who have two years' continuous service who are entitled to the 'longer' maternity absence period.

Conditions for the right to return to work

The following conditions must be met to enable the woman to return to work:

- the right to return after maternity absence applies only to employees absent from work wholly or partly because of pregnancy or childbirth (section 33 (i));

- the woman will retain her right to return whether or not the contract continues after the employee stops work (section 33(3)(i));
- to qualify for the 'longer' maternity absence period the employee must have served two years' continuous employment at the start of the eleventh week before the EWC (section 22(3)(i)(a)).

Adoption or fostering a child

These statutory rights only apply to pregnant women or those who have given birth.

Women who are adopting a child or fostering a child are not granted any statutory rights in this respect.

CHAPTER 20

Maternity Leave Period (For women with less than 2 years' service)

All employees regardless of their hours of work or their length of continuous service will be entitled to fourteen weeks' maternity leave with effect from 16 October 1994. This means that an employee would be entitled to the fourteen weeks' 'maternity leave period' if she announced that she was pregnant on her first day of work.

The maternity leave period may start any time after the eleventh week before the EWC up to the week before the EWC.

Rights during the maternity leave period

During the maternity leave period the woman will be entitled to the benefit of all her contractual rights, with the exception of remuneration, as if she had not been absent from work.

This means that contractual benefits such as holiday entitlement, company cars, pension etc, should continue to be provided during the maternity leave period.

According to *Hansard*, remuneration is to be interpreted as covering only monetary payments. This still leaves it uncertain whether 'remuneration' should also include other monetary benefits such as childcare subsidies, mortgage subsidies, luncheon vouchers, private health care such as BUPA and PPP, payment of school fees, preferential loans, payment of telephone bills etc. If it is 'remuneration' then they would cease to be applicable during the maternity leave period. If they are to be regarded as 'contractual benefits' and not 'remuneration' then they would continue to apply.

As a guide, if the benefit provided contains an element of private use, eg telephone rental, private health care, then it is more likely to be construed as a 'benefit' rather than 'remuneration'.

It may be prudent for employers to qualify the continuance of those benefits where it is questionable whether or not they should be paid during the maternity leave period by making it clear that the company reserves the right to withdraw any benefit at its discretion in the light of any future case law providing clearer guidance.

As far as pension contributions are concerned, the question is partly resolved by the Social Security Act 1989 which requires that pension benefits continue to accrue in full during 'all' paid maternity leave. This means that although the woman needs only to contribute on a pro-rata basis to the pay she receives, the employer will have to continue to make the normal employer's contribution, and if necessary, make up the shortfall in the employee's contribution, so that the employee benefits as if she had not been absent.

Period of maternity leave

The maternity leave period will end at the fourteenth week or the birth of the child, whichever is the later.

There is a compulsory period of maternity leave following the birth of the child. This means that if the baby is born late the period of leave may be extended by two weeks, or if the woman works in a factory, by four weeks.

Notification of maternity absence

The rules which a woman must follow for notifying her employer of her proposed maternity leave are exactly the same as for those employees entitled to the 'longer' maternity absence period and are described under the heading 'Notification requirements for both the maternity leave period and the "longer" maternity absence period.'

Postponement of the date of return

The employee is protected from being dismissed for a pregnancy related reason for four weeks following the end of her maternity leave period provided that she has given her employer a medical certificate prior to the end of the fourteenth week stating that she is unfit for work. (New Section 60 (d)(ii) EPCA.) This will effectively extend her maternity leave period by up to a further four weeks and any outstanding entitlement to SMP can be paid.

Returning earlier than the end of the fourteenth week

If the woman decides to return to work early then she must give at least seven days' notice in writing of her intention to her employer. If she gives less notice or no notice then the employer can postpone her return so that he will have had seven days' notice of her return. The employer cannot, however, postpone the date of return beyond the end of the fourteen week maternity leave period.

If the employee decides to return to work early despite her employer having postponed her return then the employer is under no obligation to pay her until the date of return which he has specified.

Returning at the end of the maternity leave period

The woman does not have to give any notice of her return if she is returning at the end of her maternity leave period.

The right to return to what?

Since the employee remains 'in employment' and is therefore regarded as simply on 'leave' she is entitled to return to precisely the same job which she occupied before she started her maternity absence and on exactly the same terms and conditions of employment as if she had not been absent.

Failure to return after the maternity leave period

If the employee fails to return to work at the end of the fourteenth week and the return has not been extended, either because of the late arrival of the baby or because of sickness, then employment will be assumed to have terminated by Statute.

If the employee continues to be sick after the four week extension or is unable to return because, for example, of the baby's ill health, and she is subsequently dismissed then although her statutory maternity rights will have expired, if her contract of employment is deemed to have continued to subsist, she would be entitled to notice of termination of employment and may be able to claim unfair dismissal or sex discrimination, for example if the correct policies and procedures have not been followed prior to notice being given. See *Hilton International Hotels (UK) Limited v. Kaissi (EAT 1994) IDS*.

Termination of employment during the maternity leave period

If employment is terminated during the maternity leave period, ie as a result of the employee's resignation, redundancy, the end of a fixed term contract or even as a result of gross misconduct, then entitlement to any contractual benefits will cease from the effective termination date.

Non-renewal of a fixed term contract because of pregnancy

Expiry of a fixed term contract is still a dismissal and therefore to refuse to renew it on grounds of pregnancy is automatically unfair. See *Brown v. Stockton on Tees Borough Council (1988) House of Lords*.

CHAPTER

21 Longer Maternity Absence Period

As stated above, a woman must have served two years' continuous employment at the start of the eleventh week before the EWC to qualify for the longer maternity absence period and the right to return.

This right subsists whether or not the contract ends when maternity absence begins.

Prior to the changes introduced by TURER 1993, an employee was no longer regarded as employed once she started her maternity absence unless there was anything to suggest otherwise.

This is because there are usually no further rights or obligations either for the employer or for the employee under the contract. The only rights there may be are the statutory ones such as statutory maternity pay and the right to return.

The argument that the absence constitutes termination will often be as a result of the employee's purporting to resign or the employer dismissing her.

The woman resigns

Where it is argued that the woman has resigned, the woman must have done more than merely express her intention that she does not intend to avail herself of her statutory right to return, but in due course leave her employment.

In the case of *Hughes v. Gwynedd AHA (1977) IRLR 436* the EAT held that a mere intention to leave is not an effective notice terminating her contract of employment.

Indications that the contract continues during the 'longer' maternity absence period

If there are contractual rights which continue during the "longer" maternity absence then the contract will probably be regarded as continuing:

- if the employer retains the P45 or puts the woman on a special maternity payroll this will be a strong indication that her contract did not end when her maternity leave began;
- where the absence is described as 'maternity leave' and a date of return has been agreed in advance the contract will be deemed to continue (*Lavery v. Plessey Telecommunications (1983) IRLR 202)*;
- where the woman on maternity leave was kept in the company's life assurance scheme and the company kept her P45, the Tribunal held that the contract did not end when her absence began (*Bowater Cartons Limited v. Secretary of State (Unreported))*;
- where a woman was still included in the company's sick pay scheme and received ten weeks' sick pay when she was ill during her maternity leave, the Tribunal held that her contract did not end when her absence began (*Ryan v. Sporting Tours Promotions Limited (Unreported))*;
- Even where the woman was sent her P45 on 13 July at the start

of her maternity leave she was still regarded as being employed because she was transferred to the prolonged absentees' list. Here the woman's employment was not held to have ceased until 6 November when she decided not to return to work (*Secretary of State for Employment v. Doulton Sanitaryware Limited (1981) IRLR 365).*

Options for the employer at the end of the fourteen week maternity leave period for those entitled to the longer maternity absence period

- the employer could terminate the contract with proper notice and give the contractual or statutory notice sufficiently in advance of the start of the maternity absence. The P45 would have to be sent to the woman on the effective date of termination;
- the woman could resign and would then be entitled to be given her P45;
- the woman could remain 'on contract' entitled to all her contractual terms and conditions such as sick pay, accrued holiday, continued pension contributions, death in service benefits, subsidised mortgage rates etc;
- the woman's contract could be suspended with only some of her contractual benefits applying during the maternity absence. This option could leave the employer vulnerable to an equal pay or sex discrimination claim if men are not similarly treated on similar paid/unpaid leave.

Bearing in mind that the woman's contract of employment will continue to subsist for the fourteen weeks' maternity leave period during which time all contractual benefits will be 'on' the employer needs to consider how to treat the remainder of the maternity absence where employees are entitled to the longer maternity absen period.

Although it would appear that no contractual benefits accrue during the maternity absence following the 'shorter' maternity leave period unless the employer has decided otherwise, the Tribunals no appear to be more of the view that the contract does continue to subsist during the longer absence period.

Employers may therefore be prudent to treat the woman as though she had not been absent for the whole of the 'longer' maternity absence period by allowing contractual benefits to continu to accrue throughout.

In the case of *Hilton International Hotels (UK) Limited v. Kaissi (EAT 1994) IDS Brief 517* the EAT upheld the Tribunal's finding th although Ms Kaissi had lost her statutory and contractual right to return after her maternity absence she could not automatically be deemed to have resigned when she went on maternity leave. They took the view that her contract subsisted until her employers took steps to terminate her employment which entitled her to claim that she had been unfairly dismissed.

Notification requirements

The rules for women going on both the maternity leave period and the 'longer' maternity absence period are exactly the same:

For the right to return a woman must always inform her employer in writing. If she tells her employer verbally she could los her right to return.

First notification

At least twenty-one days before the maternity leave is due to start the woman must notify her employer in writing that she will be absent because of pregnancy and that she intends to return to work.

Late notification will only be accepted by the Tribunals where it was not 'reasonably practicable' to inform before that date. For example in *Simpson v. Microponent Development (unreported)* the Tribunal accepted the woman's late notification because she had been on sick leave with complications due to her pregnancy and was ignorant of her rights.

Notification of date of return

Unlike the maternity leave period, the rules relating to the 'longer' maternity absence period are very strict and a woman who fails to comply, however insignificantly, will lose her right to return. There is no 'escape clause' for an employee if it was not reasonably practicable to notify in time.

A woman who wishes to return to work must give her employer twenty-one days' notice in writing before the end of the twenty-sixth week after the actual week of confinement, whatever the circumstances.

The twenty-nine week period runs from the actual week of childbirth (AWC), not from the expected week of childbirth (EWC). A woman must be careful to calculate the right date for her date of return particularly if the baby is born early as there may not be twenty-nine weeks from the EWC.

In *Lavery v. Plessey Telecommunications Limited (1983) IRLR 202*, Miss Lavery gave her employers only five days' notice instead of seven days' notice of her return. The Court of Appeal rejected her claim that she was entitled to return to work. One of the problems in this case was that Miss Lavery had not understood her statutory rights and her baby was born some eighteen days late. She had intended returning to work on 27 October, exactly when the twenty-nine week period would have ended had the baby arrived on time. She informed her employers on 22 October and as her employers did not want her back they refused to let her return.

As her twenty-nine week period would not have expired until 8 November, in view of the late birth, her notice would have been valid had she intended to return at that later date. However, since she failed to give the seven days' notice (formerly required by Section 47 (1) EPCA but subsequently amended by Section 11(3) EA 1980) she forfeited her right to return.

Postponement of the date of return

Similarly with the employee on the fourteen weeks' maternity leave period, the employee is able to postpone her return by up to four weeks provided that she gives her employer a doctor's certificate stating that she will be incapable of work on the notified date of return even if this means returning outside the twenty-nine week period. This four week extension can be used only once (Section 47(4) EPCA).

Unlike the employee on the fourteen weeks' maternity leave period, the employer may postpone the employee's return by up to four weeks for any reason provided he specifies it.

Also, if there is an 'interruption of work' the employer may postpone the employee's return until as soon as reasonably practicable after the interruption comes to an end (Section 47 (5) EPCA). There is no statutory definition on 'interruption of work' but it must mean industrial action because it is referred to in Section 47(5)(6) and closures due to fires, power failure or natural disasters.

Employer confirming date of return

Under Section 33(3)(A) EPCA an employer had the right to write to a woman no earlier than forty-nine days after the EWC, or actual date of birth if this is known, and ask her to confirm that she intended to return. The woman had fourteen days from receipt of that letter to confirm her intention to return.

Following TURER this letter may now be sent as early as twenty-one days before the end of the maternity leave period. This means that in theory it may be sent at around the time of the birth if the employee starts her maternity leave eleven weeks before the EWC!

It is suggested that the employer continues to write such a letter only to those employees on the 'longer' maternity absence forty-nine days after the birth as before. See draft letter Appendix 6 Page 118.

Failure to reply or replying in an ambiguous manner to this letter will mean that the woman loses her right to return. In *Betham v. Alfa Romeo (GB) Limited (1986)*, Mrs Betham replied that she could not commit herself until she knew the nature and terms of any new job offered as her job had disappeared in a re-organisation and she subsequently lost her right to return.

Weeks of accrued holiday added on

As previously stated, a woman only has the right to return any time up to the end of a twenty-nine week period starting with the week in which the baby is born. This can only be extended by the employee on medical grounds.

If there is a contractual scheme which gives the woman the right to a longer period of maternity absence then this will override her statutory rights.

If she overstays her maternity absence, whether statutory or contractual, for example by adding on accrued holiday with her employer's agreement and then fails to return, she will lose her statutory rights unless her employer is prepared to waive the rules.

In the case of *Dowuona v. John Lewis plc (1987) ICR 788*, Mrs Dowuona was very unwell after the birth of her premature twins. Her maternity absence was extended by four weeks on medical grounds and her employer agreed to add one week's holiday entitlement on the extended absence.

A letter was sent to her explaining this arrangement and confirming her revised date of return. She failed to return and subsequently her employers refused to take her back.

The Court of Appeal held that since her contract allowed for her to attach some of her holiday entitlement on to the maternity absence there had been agreement to extend her maternity absence this amount of time thus extending her period of maternity absence This meant that her failure to return on the due date deprived her of her statutory right to return and therefore her employer's refusal to allow her to return was not deemed to be a dismissal and she ha no claim.

The right to return to what?

Following the 'longer' maternity absence period the employee is entitled to return to work with her original employers or where appropriate their successor at any time before the end of the period of twenty-nine weeks beginning with the week in which the baby is actually born.

She is entitled to return to the job in which she was employed under the original contract of employment, ie the same job, same place of work, and on terms and conditions of employment not less favourable than those which would have been applicable to her if she had not been so absent (Section 45(1) EPCA). She is not entitled to a job which is more suitable to her present domestic situation.

Where it is not reasonably practicable to do so, she can be offered other suitable work on 'not substantially less favourable' terms (EPCA as amended by the Employment Act 1980). There have as yet been no cases interpreting this change.

She is entitled to treat the period of employment immediately before her maternity leave and her employment following her absence as continuous for the purposes of contractual rights such as seniority, pension rights, etc. (Section 45(2) EPCA).

The period of maternity absence itself will count for continuity purposes and for all statutory purposes (Schedule 13).

On her return she would also be entitled to receive pay reflecting any pay rises that she would have received had she not been absent.

What is the 'same' job?

It is necessary to look at the new job in terms of the nature of the work, the capacity and the place of employment to determine whether it is the same as the old job.

Nature of the work:
The nature of the work depends largely on what is specified in the contract of employment. If an employer has the right to move employees to different work then offering that different work will be lawful.

Therefore where an employer with such a right transferred a secretary to another department on her return from maternity leave it was held to be the 'same' job (*Hall v. Mather & Platt Limited*, unreported).

> *Capacity*:
> A job will not be the same as the previous job if it is in a different capacity and this includes status.

In *Berry v. BP International Limited* (unreported) it was held to be a breach of her right to return when a high powered secretary employed as personal secretary to a director was offered a job as a 'floater' on her return from maternity leave.

> *Place of Work*:
> A job is different from the previous job if the place of work is different although this will depend on whether the employer has the right under the contract of employment to move the individual.

In *Huth v. Davidson* (unreported), a secretary employed by a firm of solicitors at their office in Holloway Road was offered a job working for another partner at their office in Stamford Hill. The Tribunal held that as her contract stated that she was employed to work at their Holloway Road office this was a breach of her right to return.

CHAPTER

22 Unfair Dismissal

The right not to be unfairly dismissed

It is unlawful to dismiss an employee or to select her for redundancy because she is pregnant, or has given birth, or for any other reason connected with her pregnancy or childbirth.

It is not unlawful to dismiss an employee who is pregnant or who has recently given birth if the reasons are unrelated to her pregnancy or childbirth – unless the reasons are discriminatory or the dismissal is unfair for some other reason.

If a woman has been refused her right to return then she has the right to treat herself as dismissed and make a complaint of unfair dismissal, and if the circumstances warrant, to obtain a redundancy payment.

If a woman has been allowed to return to work but has been offered worse terms than those she would otherwise have enjoyed, then the employer would be infringing the employee's statutory maternity rights.

Employee dismissed while on maternity absence

Where a woman's contract has not been terminated and she is dismissed during maternity absence she is entitled to ignore the 'would be' dismissal and serve her s.47(1) notice, ie by giving her employer at least twenty-one days' notice of her proposal to return to work.

If she had obtained unfair dismissal compensation or redundancy payment she will be required to repay that to her employer before being allowed to return (para. 6 Schedule 2 EPCA).

In the case of *Lucas v. Norton of London (1984) IRLR 86*, Mrs Lucas did not exercise her statutory rights and her contract was not terminated when she went on maternity leave. Her employer's refusal to allow her to return amounted to a dismissal in law and the employer had to show a fair reason for dismissal. Her employer stated that the reason for dismissal was redundancy while she maintained it was because of her pregnancy. The case was remitted to a fresh Tribunal.

Dismissal of employee who tries to return

If the woman has satisfied all the conditions for the right to return, eg the service qualification and all the notification provisions, then a refusal to allow her to return will be deemed to be a dismissal taking effect from the date the woman notified as her day of return (s.56 EPCA).

If the notice requirement in s.47(1) has not been complied with, there will be no deemed dismissal (see *Lavery*).

If the employer refuses to allow a woman to return when she has failed to comply with the statutory notice provisions but has complied with the less stringent company requirements, for example by giving notice verbally or shorter notice, then she can claim unfair dismissal (*Kolfor Plant Limited v. Wright (1982) IRLR 311)*.

Complaints

An employee who believes that she has been unfairly dismissed for maternity related reasons may take her complaint to an Industrial Tribunal and make a claim of unfair dismissal.

CHAPTER

23 Contractual Maternity Schemes and Composite Rights

Statutory and contractual rights

Sometimes a woman will be subject to a contractual maternity scheme as well as the statutory scheme. A woman does not have to choose between these rights. She has a right to take advantage of a 'composite' right made up of the best terms of each scheme (s.48).

Contractual rights only

If a woman has lost her statutory rights, for example because she failed to notify her employer in accordance with s.33, she may still be able to rely on a contractual right to return and if she is prevented from returning, she may have a 'normal' unfair dismissal claim even if the dismissal occurs on her trying to return to work (*Lucas v. Norton of London Limited (1984) IRLR 86)*.

CHAPTER

24 Redundancy and Other Reasons

If an employer is unable to offer the woman her old job back because of redundancy but there is a suitable vacancy available, the employer must offer alternative employment which is suitable and appropriate to the employee in her current circumstances either in its own company, an associated employer or employer's successor (s.45(3)), otherwise the woman will be automatically treated as being unfairly dismissed (Schedule 2 para. 2(2)). The employer should not confine the search to identical or similar jobs as job share or part-time working may well be appropriate for the woman in her present condition.

In *Community Task Force v. Rimmer (1986) IRLR 203*, the EAT held that she was unfairly dismissed when she was not offered a suitable alternative post in another division of the organisation.

The job offered must be suitable in relation to the woman and the terms and conditions must not be substantially less favourable than those which would have been applicable had she not been absent (s.45(4)).

The job need not be the same but it should be similar and within the woman's capability. In *Gillespie v. The Stamping Alliance (unreported)*, her job as a comptometer operator became redundant during her maternity absence but the vacancy for a clerk in the plant department was found to be no less favourable and therefore a suitable alternative.

The terms of the alternative job need not be identical. In *Winterton v. Tony's Pharmacy (unreported)*, working on an afternoon shift instead of a morning shift was held to be suitable.

The job must be 'available' at the time the employee is due t return

The vacancy must be available at the time the employee is due to return to work. If a vacancy would have arisen at some date in the future then it would not be regarded as 'available' for the purposes o s.45 (3).

The word 'available' was defined in *Community Task Force v. Rimmer (1986) IRLR 203*, and was not restricted by the words 'economic or reasonable'. Even though the post was MSC funded with the proviso from MSC that the job-holder must be recruited from the unemployment register, the EAT held that it was still an 'available' vacancy and should have been offered to the woman on maternity absence.

What job should be offered

If there is a suitable vacancy the employer must offer employment which is 'suitable in relation to the woman and appropriate for her t do in the circumstances, and which is on terms not substantially less favourable' than those which would have applied had she not been absent (s.45(4)).

The employer need not offer all suitable vacancies. Once it is established that there was one suitable alternative vacancy the

Tribunal will examine the job actually offered to see if it meets the s.45(4) criteria.

In *Brown-Williams v. Microgen (unreported)*, the woman was one of two regional managers and while she was on maternity absence the company re-organised so that the two regional managers were to be replaced by one national manager. She was offered jobs as 'client services representative' and 'manager of the enquiry service' on the same grade and salary. The Tribunal found that there was a suitable available vacancy – that of national manager. Neither of the jobs offered was suitable and her dismissal was therefore automatically unfair under Schedule 2 Para. 2(2).

In *Gillespie v. The Stamping Alliance (unreported)*, where a job as clerk in the plant department was offered on the same pay and conditions when the job of comptometer operator was made redundant, then the Tribunal found that the requirements of s.45(4) had been satisfied.

Small firm's exemption

If the number of employees at the time immediately before the absence begins is five or less, then a breach of the right to return from 'longer' maternity absence will not amount to a dismissal in certain circumstances.

When establishing whether or not there are five or less employees, employees of an 'associated employer' are included (any two employers are treated as associated if one is a company of which the other directly or indirectly has control or both are companies of which a third person (directly or indirectly) has control (s.153(4) EPCA).

The circumstances are:

- if it was not reasonably practicable to allow her to return; and
- if it was not reasonably practicable to offer her suitable alternative employment either with her employer or with an associated employer (s.56A(1) inserted by s.12 EA1980).

In these circumstances, although the woman will technically still have the right to return, and in redundancy cases the right to be offered suitable available jobs, the result is that she will have no remedy for infringement of her rights.

This exception does not apply to women entitled only to the fourteen week maternity leave period. This means that regardless of the numbers of employees the woman will retain her right to return after fourteen weeks' maternity leave.

Non-redundancy reasons

If an employer, of whatever size, finds it is not reasonably practicable, for a non-redundancy reason, to allow the woman to return to work but:

- her employer offers her suitable alternative employment on terms not substantially less favourable than those which would have applied had she not been absent;
- which she unreasonably refuses (or accepts), then the failure to allow her to return to her old job will not be treated as a dismissal (s.56A(2) and (3)). The onus of proof is on the employer (s.56A (4)).

When is it not reasonably practicable to allow her to return?

Tribunals have held that it is not sufficient for employers to argue that they would have to dismiss the temporary replacement and therefore it was not reasonably practicable to allow the woman on maternity absence to return.

In some cases Tribunals have been persuaded that within the context of the business it is a commercial necessity to replace the woman on maternity absence with a permanent member of staff and have found the dismissal to be fair, or at least not manifestly unfair!

In *Finch v. Roussel Laboratories (unreported)*, Mrs Finch was the credit controller responsible for managing a busy and important department.

Following a spell of maternity absence she returned to work pregnant again and when she left for her second spell of maternity absence the company argued that she had to be replaced with a permanent member of staff and that it was therefore not reasonably practicable to offer her old job back.

The Tribunal was extremely sympathetic to the company and awarded Mrs Finch only her basic award.

'Suitable' alternative job offer

The formula for what is a suitable alternative job offer is the same as for a redundancy situation mentioned earlier.

Therefore, the offer of an alternative job at the Stamford Hill office of a firm of solicitors to a woman who had previously been employed at the Holloway Road office was considered substantially less favourable in view of the travelling difficulties (*Huth v. Davidsons (unreported)*).

Whereas in *Tighe v. Midland Magazine Representation Services Limited (unreported)*, during her maternity absence period the company changed its working hours to give a longer lunch break but a longer working day which the rest of the workforce accepted.

The Tribunal held that her right to return had not been infringed and that even if it had been infringed it was 'not reasonable and practicable' to allow her back on the old terms since the rest of the workforce had accepted the change and she had been offered suitable alternative employment on equally favourable terms.

Note that where a woman returns to work on substantially less favourable terms then she will have a claim for constructive dismissal.

Written reasons for dismissal

If a woman is dismissed at any time during her pregnancy or during her period of statutory maternity absence or 'longer' maternity leave then she is entitled to be given a written statement, regardless of whether she has requested it, setting out the reasons for her dismissal.

If the employer fails to provide a written statement or the employee believes that it is inaccurate or untruthful then she can take her complaint to the Industrial Tribunal.

CHAPTER

25 Pregnancy Discrimination and Equal Pay

Refusing to recruit because of pregnancy

Refusing to recruit a woman because she is pregnant amounts to direct discrimination.

In the case of *Dekker v. VJV Centrum Plus (1991) ECJ*, the ECJ held that it was direct discrimination to take an individual's sex into account when deciding whether to recruit and that as only women can be pregnant, then if pregnancy is taken into account then that too is direct discrimination. In this case Ms Dekker was the most suitable of three female candidates but because she was pregnant she was refused employment because the employer could not afford to pay her during her absence, as required under German law, and for a temporary replacement.

In Germany there is a law which prevents women who are pregnant or breastfeeding from doing overtime or nightwork between 8.00 pm and 6.00 am and if it is known at the start of the employment contract that a woman is pregnant then it can be avoided.

In *Habermann-Beltermann v. Abeiterwohlfahrt, Bezirksverband Ndb/Opf eV. (1994) ECJ*, the ECJ held that a contract of employment between an employer and a pregnant employee, both of whom were unaware that she was pregnant when the contract was entered into could not be rendered void by the employer becaus it was in contravention of the Equal Treatment Directive.

In the more recent case of *Webb v. Emo Cargo (UK) Limited (1994) ECJ*, Mrs Webb had been recruited to replace another woma who was going on maternity leave and it was anticipated by her employer that her employment would continue beyond the maternit absence period. Shortly after starting she found that she herself wa pregnant. Her employer subsequently dismissed her on the grounds of her 'inability to carry out the primary task for which she was recruited'. Following *Dekker*, the ECJ found that this was direct discrimination.

As Mrs Webb's employment had been anticipated to continue on an indefinite basis it remains unclear what the position would be if employment had been terminated on similar grounds for an employ who had been recruited solely for the period of the maternity absence.

Dismissal for pregnancy

Dismissing a woman because she is pregnant or for any reason concerned with pregnancy is automatically unfair under s.60 EPCA.

Prior to *TURER 1993* if the employer could demonstrate that the woman was incapable of doing her job because of her pregnancy or because it was illegal to continue to employ her in that job, for example if she was working with radiation, lead etc. and a suitable alternative vacancy was not available, then dismissal may have bee justified.

Following *TURER 1993* a new section, s.45, has been inserted into EPCA which provides that women who are pregnant, have recently given birth or who are breast feeding must be suspended on their full terms and conditions of employment including remuneration if they are unable to do their job as described above and there is no suitable alternative work available. This is discussed more fully later in this book.

Dismissing a pregnant woman

The EAT held that dismissing a woman because she is pregnant can constitute unlawful sex discrimination following *Hayes v. Malleable Working Men's Club.*

Mrs Hayes was a part-time barmaid at a working men's club. She became pregnant in May 1983. Up until that time her work was satisfactory but because her pregnancy was not planned this upset her to the extent that her work was affected. The club steward had received complaints that she was not pulling her weight and had told her off on several occasions for collecting glasses when she was needed for more urgent bar duties and for taking more than the normal rest breaks.

On 31 July the club steward found Mrs Hayes taking a break when the bar was particularly busy and dismissed her with one week's notice. She argued that if her employer had had complaints against a male employee they would have followed the disciplinary procedure before dismissing him. Because she had not been treated on that basis she claimed that she had been discriminated against on the grounds of her sex.

Discriminating in terms and conditions during maternity

Those employers who opt to suspend the contract, and therefore all the terms and conditions, during the 'longer' maternity absence and after the first fourteen weeks of leave should be aware that if they d not make such arrangements for men who go on unpaid leave, they may be discriminating on grounds of sex or offending against the Equal Pay Act.

In *Coyne v. Export Credits Guarantee Department (1981) IRLR 51*, Mrs Coyne succeeded in her claim for equal pay when she was excluded from her employer's sick pay scheme during her unpaid maternity leave.

In *Reay v. Sunderland Health Authority (1993) IDS Brief 487*, the Tribunal held that it was discriminatory to allow male nurses on sick leave to accrue additional holidays to compensate for the bank holidays that occurred whilst they were on sick leave but did not allow this benefit to women on maternity absence. Cases such as this imply that the Tribunals are already looking towards employers granting benefits during absence.

Refusing to allow women on maternity absence to return part-time

To refuse to allow a woman to return to part-time working following her maternity absence may be indirect discrimination unless employers can show that there are good business reasons to justify their requirements.

In *The Home Office v. Holmes (1984) IRLR 299*, Ms Holmes was refused her request to return to work on a part-time basis following her maternity absence. The Home Office claimed that her only right was to return to her full-time job and that there were no part-time posts in her grade.

Ms Holmes claimed that by refusing to allow her to return part-time this was indirect discrimination since far fewer women could comply with the requirement to work full-time. The EAT upheld her claim on the grounds that the Home Office could not justify their requirement for full-time working only.

It should also be borne in mind that to refuse to allow a man who is the 'carer' the opportunity to go part-time or to job-share may be discriminatory unless there are good reasons for the refusal.

CHAPTER

26 Health and Safety

Pregnant Workers Directive 1992

The Pregnant Workers Directive is concerned with the whole of pregnancy and maternity and the health of the child and therefore provides protection for women both while they are pregnant, after they have given birth and while they are breastfeeding.

These new provisions, which must have been in place by 16 October 1994, will have already been put in place partly by *TURERA 1993*, through Regulations to be issued by the Health and Safety Commission and by the new Statutory Maternity Pay rules introduced by the DSS.

The right to be offered suitable alternative work

Schedule 3 s.46 *TURERA 1993* provides that employees who are pregnant, have recently given birth or are breast feeding should be offered any suitable alternative work if they are unable to continue in their jobs on maternity related health and safety grounds.

The alternative work offered must be suitable to the employee and appropriate for her to undertake in her condition as an employee who is pregnant, has recently given birth or is breastfeeding. If the terms and conditions of the work offered differ from those of her normal job then they must not be 'substantially less favourable'.

If an employee unreasonably refuses an offer of alternative work then she will not be entitled to be paid for the period of her suspension.

Medical Suspension

If there is no suitable alternative work available then the employee must be suspended and she will be entitled to receive the same remuneration and benefits as if she had not been suspended.

An employee who is on medical suspension may choose to start her maternity leave any time from the eleventh week before the EWC up to the week before the EWC.

Complaints

An employee may take her complaint to a Tribunal if her employer has failed to pay part or all of the remuneration due to her following her suspension on maternity related health and safety grounds.

The complaint must normally be lodged within three months from the first day that payment was not made. If the complaint is well-founded then the employer will be ordered to pay any remuneration due to the woman.

Health and Safety Regulations

The Management of Health and Safety at Work Regulations 1992 already require employers to:

> 'assess the risks to the health and safety of their employees . . . . . .';
> and
> 'give employees information about the risks to their health and safety identified by the assessment'.

The Regulations are to be amended to incorporate the health and safety requirements of the Pregnant Workers Directive as follows:

> The employee will be required to inform her employer that she is either pregnant, has recently given birth or is breastfeeding following which her employer is required to take certain measures to safeguard her health and safety.

Assessment:

> An assessment of the woman's working conditions must be carried out to determine whether there is any potential risk to her health and safety. This should include an assessment of the physical, biological and chemical hazards in the individual's workplace which may create potential risks.

Annex 1 of the Directive provides a non-exhaustive list of the 'agents, processes and working conditions' which must be included in the assessment. See Appendix 8, page 123.

This assessment may already have been undertaken under the Management of Health and Safety at Work Regulations and provided that this remains valid and account has been taken of the risks to the new or expectant mother, this will be adequate.

The results of the assessment and any measures to be taken must be notified to the employee.

Adjustment of working conditions:

> If the assessment reveals a risk to the health and safety of the woman then there must be a temporary adjustment to her working conditions and/or working hours so that she is not exposed to the risk.

If it is not possible to make a temporary adjustment to her working conditions then she must be offered suitable alternative work. If suitable alternative work cannot be found then she must be given paid leave for as long a period as is necessary for health and safety reasons.

Specific risks:

Annex II of the Directive provides a non-exhaustive list of 'specific risks' which are harmful to the pregnant employee and the employee who is breastfeeding and they should therefore not be exposed to them. See Appendix 8.

Night Work:

On production of a medical certificate stating that it is necessary for their health and safety, women employed on night work have the right to be transferred to suitable daytime work during their pregnancy and for a certain period of time after childbirth. If that is not possible then they must be given paid leave.

Appendices

1. Legislation Affecting SMP and Maternity Rights
2. Form SMP 1
3. State Maternity Allowance and SMP (1994/95)
4. Maternity Certificate
5. Termination Dates
6. Draft Example Letters
7. Action Checklist
8. Non-exhaustive List of Agents, Processes and Working Conditions

Appendix 1

Legislation Affecting SMP and Maternity Rights

Employment Protection (Consolidation) Act 1978 as amended.

Social Security Act 1986.

The Statutory Maternity Pay (General) Regulations 1986.

The Statutory Maternity Pay (Medical Evidence) Regulations 1987.

The Social Security (Adjudication) Regulations 1986.

Maternity Pay and Maternity Allowance (Transitional) Regulations 1987.

Statutory Maternity Pay (Person Abroad and Mariners) Regulations 1987.

Sex Discrimination Act 1975.

Social Security Act 1989.

Statutory Maternity Pay (General) Amendment Regulations 1990.

Appendix 2

SMP Statutory Maternity Pay

Surname: Mrs/Miss/Ms

Other names

Address

NI number: Letters | Numbers | Letter

Works or clock number

Why I cannot pay you SMP (Statutory Maternity Pay)

I have ticked the box which applies to you

☐ I cannot pay you SMP. The back of this letter shows why I cannot pay you.

☐ I cannot pay you any more SMP after the week which ends on Saturday / /

You are entitled to ____ weeks SMP from me until then. The back of this letter shows why I cannot carry on paying you.

What to do if you disagree
If you disagree with this decision please ask me about it. If you still disagree you can ask your local Social Security office for advice.

Maternity Allowance
You may be able to get Maternity Allowance from your Social Security office.

Ask your ante-natal clinic or Social Security office for a leaflet about Maternity Allowance.

How to claim Maternity Allowance

1 Get claim form MA 1 from your ante-natal clinic or your local Social Security office.

2 Fill in claim form MA 1.

3 Send claim form MA 1 to your local Social Security office with this letter and your Maternity Certificate form Mat B1. If you gave me your Maternity Certificate I have given it back with this letter.

If you want to ask me anything about this letter please let me know.

Employer's signature

Employer's name and address

Telephone number

Date / /

Form SMP 1

Why I cannot pay you SMP

I have ticked the box or boxes which tell you why I cannot pay you SMP.

☐	**You were not employed by me for long enough**	to get SMP you must be employed by me for at least 26 weeks in a row into the 15th week before your baby is due. You would not have been employed by me for long enough even if ► I dismissed you before the 15th week before your baby was due because you were pregnant or ► you left my employment because you had your baby before the 15th week before the date your baby was due
☐	**Your earnings were too low**	to get SMP your average earnings must be enough to pay National Insurance contributions on.
☐	**You did not tell me soon enough that you would be away from work**	to get SMP you must give me at least 3 weeks notice that you will be away from work because you are pregnant. You did not have a good reason for giving me less notice than this.
☐	**You did not give me medical evidence soon enough**	to get SMP you must give me your Maternity Certificate (form Mat B1), or other acceptable evidence, within 3 weeks of the beginning of your Maternity Pay Period. If you had a good reason for taking longer than this I could only allow you up to 13 weeks to give me this evidence.
☐	**You did not tell me soon enough that you had had your baby**	to get SMP you must tell me about your baby within 3 weeks of the date your baby is born. If you had a good reason for taking longer than this I could only allow you up to 13 weeks to tell me.
☐	**You were out of the European Community**	you cannot get SMP if you are out of the European Community at the beginning of your Maternity Pay Period. If you have been getting SMP you stop getting it when you leave the European Community.
☐	**You were in legal custody**	you cannot get SMP if you are in legal custody at the beginning of your Maternity Pay Period. If you have been getting SMP you stop getting it when you go into legal custody.

Some important dates that affect your entitlement to SMP

1 **The week your baby is due**	The first day of that week is	/ /
2 **The week that is 15 weeks before the week your baby is due**	The first day of that week is	/ /
3 **Your Maternity Pay Period**	Your Maternity Pay Period is the period during which you could get SMP. Your Maternity Pay Period begins on or would have begun on	/ /

Printed in the UK for HMSO Dd 8041932 52-6517 2632M 1/87 CPL

Appendix 3

State Maternity Allowance and SMP (1994/95)

Current State Maternity Allowance	SMP
Eligibility for employees:	
1 Have worked as an employee or been self employed for at least twenty-six weeks in the sixty-six weeks ending with the week before the EWC.	1 Twenty-six weeks' service with the same employer ending with the fifteenth week before the EWC.
2 Have paid contributions of a relevant class for at least twenty-six weeks in the sixty-six weeks ending with the week before the EWC and in the case of Class 1 contributions to have paid these at the full rate.	2 The last eight weeks' average earnings must be at or above LEL.
	3 Employee must reach fifteenth week before EWC or have given birth.
Duration:	
Up to eighteen weeks.	Higher rate:
Working women have some flexibility over the start date but	The first six weeks are paid at 90% of average earnings

it cannot start any earlier than the eleventh week before the EWC or later than the week after the week of childbirth.	Lower rate: Up to twelve weeks at a rate set by the State.
Current rate:	
Standard rate is £52.50 if employed at the eleventh week before the EWC for women whose babies were due on or after 16 October 1994.	Higher rate SMP is based on 90% of average earnings. Lower rate for employees whose EWC was on or after 16 October 1994 is £52.50. Both are subject to tax and NIC.
Claim from DSS	**Claim from employer**

Note: Different qualifying conditions and a different rate of SMA apply to those individuals claiming SMA who are self-employed or non-employed.

Appendix 4

Form Mat B1

MATERNITY CERTIFICATE

Please fill in this form in ink

Name of patient ____________________________

TO THE PATIENT

Please read the notes on the back of this form ▶

Part A

Fill in this part if you are giving the certificate ***before*** *the confinement*

Do not fill this in more than 14 weeks before the expected week of confinement

I certify that I examined you on the date given below and in my opinion you can expect to be confined in

the week that includes / /

Part B

Fill in this part if you are giving the certificate ***after*** *the confinement*

I certify that I attended you in connection with

your confinement which took place on / /

when you were delivered of a child (____ children)

Fill in the rest of Part B if the birth was before the expected week of confinement

In my opinion your confinement was expected in

the week that includes / /

Date of examination / /

Date of signing / /

Signature

Registered midwives
please give your registered number or address here

THIS IS YOUR MATERNITY CERTIFICATE

for you to use if you claim

- Statutory Maternity Pay (SMP)
- Maternity Benefits

Before you use the certificate, please fill in your name and address

Your full name ____________________________

Your address and postcode ____________________________

More information

You can get leaflet FB8 about 'Babies and Benefits' from ante-natal clinics. You can also get this leaflet, and others, from any Social Security office, where you can also get advice about which benefits you can claim.
You will find their phone number and address in the phone book under HEALTH & SOCIAL SECURITY or SOCIAL SECURITY.

There are time limits for claiming. You may lose money if your claim is late.

Statutory Maternity Pay (SMP)

You may be entitled to SMP from your employer if

- you have worked for one employer from the beginning of your pregnancy into the 15th week before your expected date of confinement.

Ask your employer if you can get SMP. Do this now.

Maternity Allowance

This is a benefit you may be entitled to if

- you are self-employed
- you do not have an employer
- your employer cannot pay you SMP.

If you think you may be entitled to Maternity Allowance get a claim form MA 1 from a Social Security office now.

Child Benefit

You can claim this benefit when your baby is born. Use the coupon in the 'Babies and Benefits' leaflet to get a claim form. Or write to your Social Security office for one - they will need to know if you are already getting Child Benefit.

Maternity Payment from the social fund

You may be able get this payment if

- you or your partner are getting Supplementary Benefit or Family Income Supplement.

Get form SF 100 from your ante-natal clinic or Social Security office. When you claim you may use this certificate or some other proof, like your clinic appointment card.

Appendix 5

Termination Dates

1. Where the employee confirms that she does not wish to return, the date of termination will be at the end of the period of SMP entitlement.

2. Where the employee, before commencing leave, has indicated her intention to return to work but subsequently notifies you that she will not be returning, the date of termination will be the date of the notification of not returning, provided this is after the end of the period of SMP entitlement.

3. Where the employee, before commencing leave, indicates her intention to return to work but subsequently declines to confirm that intention during absence, the effective date of termination will be the deadline for complying with the company's request for confirmation, ie fourteen days after the employee receives the letter, unless it was not reasonably practicable for the employee to reply.

4. Where the employee, before commencing leave, indicates her intention to return to work but fails to notify a date of return within twenty-six weeks after the commencement of the week of the birth of the baby, the effective date of termination will be the end of the period of absence, ie twenty-nine weeks after the beginnning of the week of the birth.

5. Where the employee, before commencing leave, indicates her intention to return but fails to notify a date of return because there is an interruption of work which renders it unreasonable to expect the employee to return to work before the expiry of the twenty-nine weeks after the beginning of the week of the birth, the effective date of termination will be the end of the period of twenty-eight days from the end of the period of interruption of work.
6. Where the employee notifies in writing within twenty-six weeks after the commencement of the week of the birth of the baby, a date of return not less than twenty-one days hence, but fails to return on that notified date, the effective date of termination of employment will be that notified date, unless it was not reasonably practicable for the employee to return on that date.
7. Where the employee notifies in writing within twenty-six weeks after the commencement of the week of the birth of the baby, a date of return not less than twenty-one days hence, but cannot return to her original job because of redundancy and is not redeployed, the date of termination will be the notified date of return. This date will be later in the event of an unsuccessful trial period.

Note: Following cases such as *Hilton International Hotels (UK) Limited v. Kaissi (EAT 1994)*, the courts are likely to take the view that the contract continues to susbsist during the period of maternity absence and therefore if the employer takes steps to terminate the employment relationship, care should be taken to follow the appropriate procedures otherwise the employee may be able to claim that she was unfairly dismissed.

Appendix 6

Draft Example Letters

Letter confirming notification requirements

To: (*Company*)

From: (*Employee's name, address, payroll number*)

I confirm my intention to commence maternity leave on (*date*) and that I will/will not be returning to work after the birth of my child.

Attached is a copy of my certificate of expected date of childbirth (form MAT B1) and I will inform you of the actual date of birth at the earliest opportunity.

I understand that the company may write to me, no earlier than twenty-one days before the end of the 'fourteenth week' period of maternity leave, seeking confirmation of my intentions and that I will lose the right to return if I do not reply within fourteen days to such a request confirming my intention to return to work.

I also understand that I may postpone my return for up to four weeks on certified medical grounds and that the company may, at its discretion, postpone my return from the 'longer' maternity absence period for up to four weeks.

I further understand that I have the right to return to my original job. However, in the event that this is not available, following 'longer' maternity absence, that I may be offered suitable alternative employment on terms which are not substantially less favourable than the terms which would have applied if I had not been on leave.

Signed by employee...Date...............................

Confirmation of return to work

To be sent by recorded delivery no sooner than twenty-one days before the end of the fourteen week maternity leave period but ideally no sooner than fourty-nine days after the EWC or beginning of the notified date of childbirth if sooner.

(*Headed notepaper of employer*)

Dear (*Employee*)

(*Start letter by offering congratulations on the birth of the child!*)

Further to your letter of (*date*) concerning your maternity leave, will you please confirm in writing that it is still your intention to return to work. A stamped addressed envelope is enclosed for your reply.

Please understand that your right to resume employment will be lost if you do not comply with this request within fourteen days from receipt of this letter.

Yours sincerely

Letter to temporary replacement

(Suggested paragraph to be included in offer letter to temporary replacement for an employee on maternity leave)

Our offer of employment is on a temporary basis to cover the period that our employee is away for maternity reasons. We anticipate that the duration of your employment is likely to be for around (*x*) months/weeks and will be terminated with due notice on the employee's return from maternity absence.

Appendix 7

Action Checklist

- Decide whether the fourteen weeks' maternity leave should be extended to eighteen weeks to mirror the Statutory Maternity Pay Period;
- Decide what benefits are 'contractual' and should therefore continue to be enjoyed during the fourteen week maternity leave period;
- Compare the rights and benefits enjoyed by those on sick leave with those on maternity leave;
- Decide whether to extend the contractual benefits beyond the fourteen weeks' maternity absence to cover the full 'longer' maternity leave period;
- If benefits are not to be extended to the 'longer' maternity absence period decide how the woman will be informed;
- If benefits are to be extended consider whether some should be enjoyed on a discretionary basis until such time as case law has established whether or not they should be classified as 'remuneration' or 'benefits';
- Assess the health and safety risks of all jobs in the light of a woman who is pregnant, has recently given birth or who is breastfeeding;
- Identify ways of altering duties or giving instructions so that any risks can be removed;

- Identify suitable alternative work to offer women who are at risk due to maternity related reasons;
- Update maternity policy, standard letters and checklists in light of revised maternity provisions;
- Review potential for jobs traditionally undertaken on a full-time basis to be undertaken on a part-time basis so that genuine consideration can be given to women returners requesting part-time working arrangements;
- Check disciplinary and redundancy procedures;
- Ensure that management are trained in the new rules and procedures.

Appendix 8

Non-exhaustive List of Agents, Processes and Working Conditions

Referred to in Article 4(1) of EC Directive on Pregnant Workers

A. Agents

1. *Physical agents* where these are regarded as agents causing foetal lesions and/or likely to disrupt placental attachment, and in particular:

   (a) shocks, vibration or movement;

   (b) handling of loads entailing risks, particularly of a dorsolumbar nature;

   (c) noise;

   (d) ionizing radiation;

   (e) non-ionizing radiation;

   (f) extremes of cold or heat;

   (g) movements and postures, travelling – either inside or outside the establishment – mental and physical fatigue and other physical burdens connected with the activity of the worker within the meaning of Article 2 of the Directive.

2. *Biological agents*

   Biological agents of risk groups 2, 3 and 3 within the meaning of Article 2(d) numbers 2, 3 and 4 of Directive 90/679/EEC, in so far as it is known that these agents or the therapeutic measures necessitated by such agents endanger the health of pregnant women and the unborn child and in so far as they do not yet appear in Annex II.

3. *Chemical agents*

   The following chemical agents in so far as it is known that they endanger the health of pregnant women and the unborn child ar in so far as they do not yet appear in Annex II:

   (a) substances labelled R 40, R 45, R 46, and R 47 under Directive 67/548/EEC in so far as they do not yet appear in Annex II;

   (b) chemical agents in Annex I to Directive 90/394/EEC;

   (c) mercury and mercury derivatives;

   (d) antimitotic drugs;

   (e) carbon monoxide;

   (f) chemical agents of known and dangerous percutaneous absorption.

B. Processes

Industrial processes listed in Annex I to Directive 90/394/EEC.

C. Working conditions

Underground mining work.

Referred to in Article 6 of EC Directive on Pregnant Workers

A. Pregnant workers within the meaning of Article 2(a)

1. *Agents*

   (a) Physical agents
   Work in hyperbaric atmosphere, eg pressurized enclosures and underwater diving.

   (b) Biological agents
   The following biological agents:
   — toxoplasma,
   — rubella virus,
   unless the pregnant workers are proved to be adequately protected against such agents by immunization.

   (c) Chemical agents
   Lead and lead derivatives in so far as these agents are capable of being absorbed by the human organism.

2. *Working conditions*
   Underground mining work.

D. Workers who are breastfeeding within the meaning of Article 2(c).

1. *Agents*

   (a) Chemical agents
   Lead and lead derivatives in so far as these agents are capable of being absorbed by the human organism.

2. *Working conditions*
   Underground mining work.